Weather

by Tim

What makes up weather?

Parts of Weather

Weather is what the air is like outside. The air temperature is part of the weather. So is the water in the air. The wind speed and kinds of clouds are part of the weather too.

Clouds are made of water droplets. Clouds hang in the air. When a cloud can't hold any more water, it rains. Puffy, white clouds usually mean good weather. Dark clouds usually bring rain.

Measuring Weather

You might say that the weather is hot today. But your friend might disagree. To your friend, the weather might not feel hot. So scientists use tools to measure the weather. That way, we know exactly what the weather is like!

Earth has a blanket of air around it. That blanket is called the **atmosphere.** It contains gases that have no color, taste, or odor. The atmosphere has weight. It presses down on Earth. How much it presses down is called air pressure. High air pressure is caused by the atmosphere pressing down more. Low air pressure is caused by the atmosphere pressing down less.

The atmosphere has many parts. Weather happens in the lower part. Planes often fly above the weather.

Changes in air pressure lead to changes in the weather. Scientists use a tool called a barometer to measure air pressure.

High air pressure means good weather is coming or is here. The skies are clear or will be clearing. Low air pressure often means bad weather. The weather is cloudy or rainy or will be cloudy or rainy. Storms happen during low air pressure.

Barometer

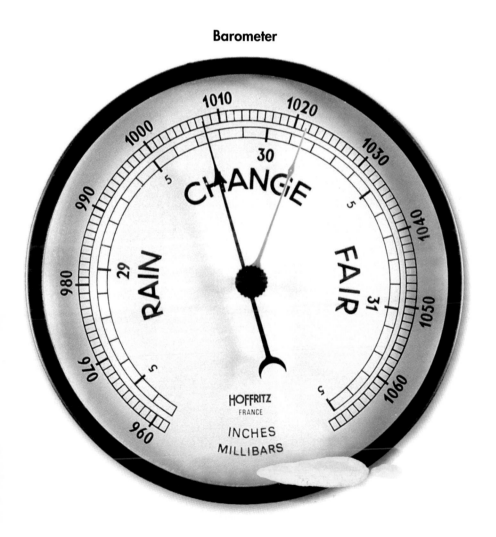

Hygrometer

A hygrometer measures the air's water vapor, or humidity. High humidity causes damp, wet air. Low humidity causes dry air.

A rain gauge shows how much rain has fallen. An anemometer tells the speed of the wind. Wind vanes tell the direction of the wind.

All these tools help scientists predict what the weather will be like.

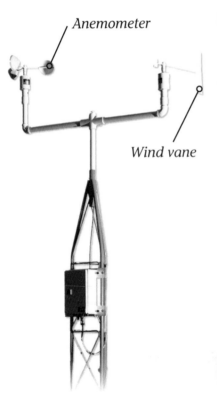

Anemometer

Wind vane

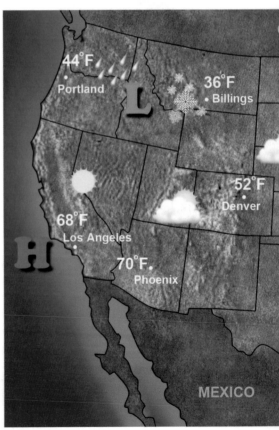

44°F
Portland

36°F
• Billings

52°F
• Denver

68°F
Los Angeles

70°F.
Phoenix

MEXICO

Weather Map

Weather tools give scientists data, or facts. Scientists use the data to make weather maps. The maps show temperatures, air pressure, and storms. Look closely at the weather map below. Do you see the key? The key's pictures help you better understand the weather.

This weather map uses pictures to show what the weather is like. What is the weather like in Atlanta, Georgia?

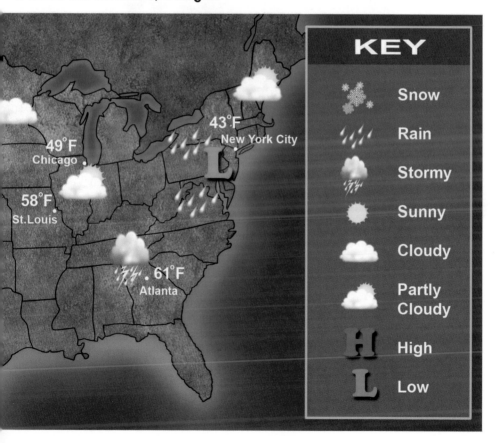

Weather satellites move around Earth and take pictures. They send the pictures back to Earth. Scientists study the pictures. The pictures help scientists tell which way storms are moving. This helps scientists talk about the weather.

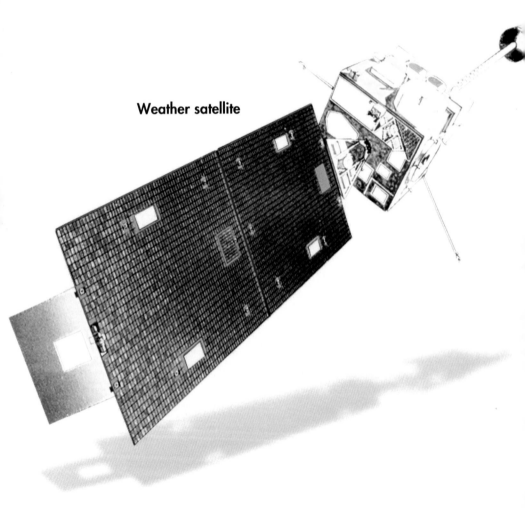

Weather satellite

Smog makes it hard for some people to breathe.

Pollution Alerts

Cars, trucks, and factories can pollute the air in cities. The pollution they make is a gas, called exhaust. The exhaust moves into the air. The exhaust can hang over the city. The Sun's rays can turn the exhaust into smog and ozone.

Weather scientists make pollution alerts when there's smog or ozone in the air. The alerts warn people to stay inside because smog or ozone can be harmful to health.

How does weather affect people?

Weather Patterns

Weather changes follow patterns. The same weather happens over and over again. Weather patterns depend on the Sun, water, and where you live. People near the ocean have one kind of weather. People far from the ocean have another kind of weather.

The coast of Washington State has rainy winters. The Cascade Mountains, near the middle of the state, have snowy winters. And eastern Washington State has dry, cold winters.

Eastern Washington State does not get much rain or snow.

What kind of weather does this desert have?

It rains on the coast because the air is warm and wet. The rain turns to snow in the mountains because the air is colder there. And the mountains block rain and snow from going past them.

All deserts are dry. Some deserts are hot. Others are cold. The Sonoran Desert in Southern Arizona and California has a rainy summer season. The rain comes from moist air from the Gulf of California. Saguaro cactus take in the rain and save it for later.

11

Dangerous Storms

Some storms only bring rain. Thunderstorms can be dangerous. Lightning can strike people, trees, and buildings, so people should find shelter.

A **hurricane** is a huge storm. It starts out over an ocean. It has very strong winds. When it hits the land it causes great damage. People usually know about hurricanes before they happen.

A hurricane can cause heavy rain and huge waves.

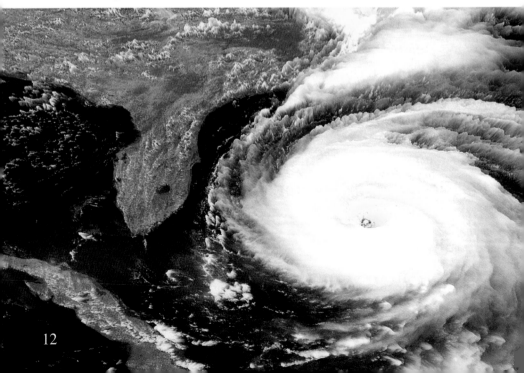

A tornado is very dangerous.

A **tornado** is a spinning column of air that touches the ground. Tornadoes form below thunderstorm clouds. They are smaller than hurricanes. But their winds are much stronger. Tornados form quickly. When a tornado is spotted, people must go to a safe place.

Heavy rains or big waves can cause flooding. Flooding can make roads dangerous to travel on. People usually know about flooding beforehand and move to higher ground.

A **blizzard** is a winter storm. Blizzards have very cold air and a lot of snow. Strong winds blow the snow. It is dangerous to be out in a blizzard. Blizzards can trap people in the snow. They can also make people too cold. It is important to stay indoors during blizzards in order to be safe.

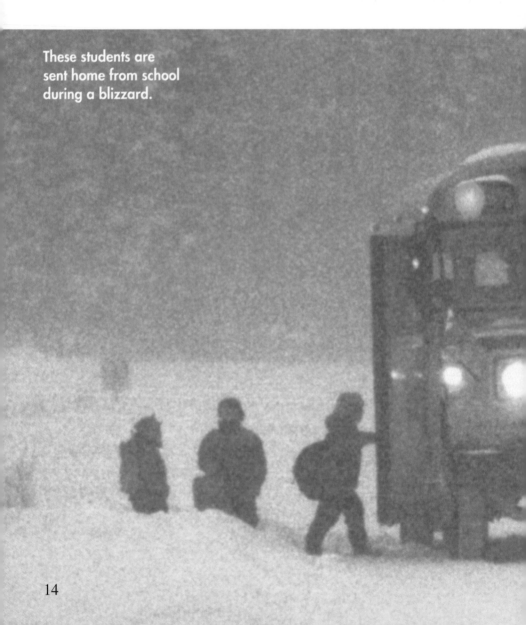

These students are sent home from school during a blizzard.

The National Weather Service warns people about storms. A storm watch means that a storm could be happening soon. A storm warning means that a storm is about to happen or is already happening.

Different kinds of weather happen every day. It is difficult to figure out why certain weather happens. But tools help scientists understand the weather!

Glossary

atmosphere   the mixture of gases and air that surrounds Earth.

blizzard   a very heavy snowstorm with strong winds and very cold temperatures.

hurricane   a huge storm with strong winds and very heavy rains that starts over an ocean.

tornado   a spinning, funnel-shaped column of air that touches the ground.

weather   what the air is like outside.

What did you learn?

1. What are some qualities that weather has?

2. Name three weather tools that help to measure weather. Tell what each tool does.

3. What do high air pressure and low air pressure tell us about the weather?

4. **Writing** in Science In this book you have read about the pollution that happens in cities. Write to explain how pollution forms. Use examples from the book.

5. **Make Inferences** Why do you think Washington State's coast gets wet weather in the winter, while the Cascade Mountains in the middle of the state, get snow?

Genre	Comprehension Skill	Text Features	Science Content
Nonfiction	Make Inferences	• Captions • Map • Labels • Glossary	Weather

Scott Foresman Science 3.6

scottforesman.com

ISBN 0-328-13823-1

90000

9 780328 138234

CO–CRAZY

One Psychologist's Recovery from Codependency and Addiction

A MEMOIR & ROADMAP TO FREEDOM

SARAH MICHAUD, PsyD